AF456027

Table of Contents

Introduction

Bread is generally viewed as a perishable commodity, while in its many forms is one of the most staple foods consumed by humans, that`s shelf life is limited by two main factors, including staling and microbial (fungi spoilage and ropiness) attack (Katina, 2005; Arendt et al., 2007).

Preservation of foods by fermentation is a widely practiced and ancient technology. There has been much interest in the potential application of Lactic Acid Bacteria (LAB) as a means of biopreservation that is control of one organism by another (Clarke and Arendt, 2005).

The use of sourdough process as a form of leavening is one of the oldest biotechnological processes in food production that have been used for thousands of years and are generally regarded as safe. Traditional acidic sourdough is ancient way to improve flavour, texture and microbiological shelf life of bread that is used in Mediterranean countries. Today, sourdough baking is an alternative to the use of additives (Katina, 2005).

Sourdough is a very complex biological system and is an important modern fermentation method of cereal flours (especially Rye and Wheat) and water that is fermented with certain microorganisms. A common trend of sourdough fermentations is the unique symbiosis of certain hetero and homo fermentative lactic acid bacteria with certain yeasts. The interaction of yeasts and lactobacilli is important for the metabolic activity of sourdough. Several yeasts are found in sourdoughs but Saccharomyces cerevisiae is considered the dominant organism for leavening of bread. The most relevant bacteria isolated from sourdough belong to the genus Lactobacillus and the rheology, flavour, nutritional and functional properties of sourdough based baked products greatly rely on the activity of these microorganisms. Lactic acid bacteria usually originate from flour, dough ingredients or the environment (De Vuyst and Neysens, 2005; Gobbetti et al., 2005; Paramithiotis et al., 2006; Corsetti and Settanni, 2007).

LAB to yeast ratio in sourdoughs is generally 100:1. Whereas in the majority of fermented foods homo fermentative LAB play an important role, hetero fermentative LAB are dominating in sourdough, especially when traditionally prepared. The dominance of obligate hetero fermentative lactobacilli in sourdoughs can be explained mainly by their competitiveness and adaptation to this particular environment. The importance of antagonistic and synergistic interactions between lactobacilli and yeasts are based on the metabolism of carbohydrates and amino acids and the production of carbon dioxide (Gobbetti, 1998; Clarke et al., 2004; Corsetti et al., 2007).

Commercial sourdough processes do not rely on fortuitous flora but on the use of commercial starter cultures. Inoculation of the sourdough with starters increases the number of lactic acid bacteria to 107-108 cfu g-1, which gives little possibility for growth of contaminating organisms. The range of commercial starter culture includes pure starter cultures in powder form and starter cultures that are active sourdoughs. Sourdough fermentation is based on lactic acid and alcoholic fermentation depending on the composition of microflora and fermentation conditions (fermentation temperature, time and dough yield). These factors do not act separately but in an interactive way, adding to the complexity of the system (Thiele, 2003; Katina, 2005).

Sourdoughs have been classified into three types, based on the kind of technology applied for their production, as used in artisan and industrial processes. Type I sourdoughs are manufactured by traditional techniques and are characterized by continuous (daily) propagation to keep the microorganisms in an active metabolic state. Generally, three stage fermentation processes are used at a temperature below 30 °C. Type II sourdoughs involve a less time consuming, one stage fermentation process at a temperature exceeding 30 °C and are used mostly in industrial processes. Sourdoughs are fermented for a long period (up to 5 days) with a high dough yield (semi liquid preparation) and microorganisms show restricted metabolic activity. Sourdoughs serve mainly as dough acidifiers and flavouring agents. Type III sourdoughs are manufactured by sourdough fermentation with subsequent water evaporation leading to dried preparations which are used as acidifier supplements and aroma carriers (Meignen et al., 2001; De Vuyst and Neysens, 2005; Gaggiano et al., 2007).

Sourdough fermentations enhance dough properties; improve volume, texture, flavour, retard the staling process of bread and protect bread from mould and bacterial spoilage (Katina et al., 2002; De Vuyst and Vancanneyt, 2007).

Some of the reported benefits of sourdough on bread quality may be based on the formation of exopolysaccharides by certain lactic acid bacteria, whereas most of the beneficial properties attributed to sourdough are determined by the acidification activity of lactic acid bacteria. Sourdough LAB fermentation creates an optimum pH for the activity of endogenous factors

(Thiele et al., 2002) which improves texture changes (Clarke et al., 2004), contributes directly to bread flavour, especially, through the synthesis of acetic acid (Gobbetti et al., 2005; Ur-Rehman et al., 2006), increases the loaf volume (Corsetti et al., 1998), delays starch retrogradation and bread firming (Katina, 2005) and inhibits ropiness by spore-forming bacteria (Messens and De Vuyst, 2002; Simsek et al., 2006; Mentes et al., 2007).

Meanwhile exopolysaccharides produced by sourdough lactic acid bacteria exert effects such as cholesterol lowering, immunomodulating, antitumoral and prebiotic activities. Many new interesting applications for sourdough remain still to be explored, such as the use of prebiotic starter cultures or production of totally new types of bioactive compounds. Furthermore, recent results demonstrate that sourdough fermentation can improve texture and palatability of whole grain, fiber rich or gluten free products, stabilize or increase levels of various bioactive compounds, reduced amounts of harmful compounds, improve mineral and retard starch bioavailability (low glyceamic index products). Pre fermentation of wheat bran with lactic acid bacteria in sourdough bread improved phytate breakdown (up to 90%) and increased magnesium and phosphorus solubility (Katina et al., 2005).

There has also been much progress in the development of tools that allow for the selection of key sourdough microorganisms for particular activities such as those concerned with enzymatic, antifungal, antimicrobial, nutritional and additive replacement aspects.

WHAT IS SOURDOUGH ?

Basically, it's how people used to make bread and other baked goods "rise" before there were those handy packets of yeast or containers of baking powder at the local stores. Before these were available (around 1850), the way to "leaven" bread was by adding some sourdough "starter" to the dough and allowing it to rise over time.

Because sourdough has been around for a long time, nobody really knows how it started. Most people believe it began after someone mixed flour and water to get ready for baking, and left the mixture around for too long. After a while, they noticed that it started to expand. When they saw this happen and then baked it, they noticed the bread was lighter and easier to eat.

Then, people found that if they saved some of the unbaked dough after it had risen, and mixed it with the next batch of bread, it would rise more quickly. This unbaked dough could also be split to share with other people, and it became known as a sourdough starter.

Let's start with the basics, as you probably want to make a sourdough starter from scratch. I will explain a few differences in terminology here, but if you want to go straight to the process for making a sourdough starter from scratch.

What is a sourdough starter?

Something quite incredible happens when you mix flour and water together. This mixture begins to absorb wild yeasts and bacteria from the environment, and the more you refresh it (refreshing your starter means you are keeping some of it, and adding fresh flour and water to it), the stronger and more active it will become. Ultimately, it will become so potent that you can make your bread rise in the oven. The period between refreshments is called fermentation, and thus when you use your starter to make bread you are using "pre-fermented" flour in your mix.

What do I call it?: Many people might give their sourdough starter a name, but that's not what I'm getting at here. Let's talk about the names and terms used in regards to sourdough, as these terms can be interchangeable yet they seem to confuse lots of beginners:

Sourdough vs Naturally Leavened

If you tell me that your bread is sourdough, the first thing that comes to my mind is that you have fermented your dough for a long period of time and that you used pre-fermented flour to make your bread rise, aka your sourdough starter. If you tell me your bread is naturally leavened, well, I'd think the same thing! These two terms are often used to designate the fact that a loaf of bread was made with a fermented mixture of flour and water - a sourdough starter.

Feel free to use them interchangeably.

Sourdough Starter vs Levain

When your sourdough starter is ready to use after you make it from scratch, it is now known to be active. An active starter indicates it is healthy and when fed it will reach a point where you can add it to your final dough mix to begin the process of making bread. When it is at the point to where it rises and is ready for your final dough mix, your starter is now commonly referred to as a levain or a leaven (French and English words that mean to make something rise). After this peak point passes, your levain will start to decline in size and lose strength. Usually around 13-14 hours after you fed your starter, it will return back to the same state as prior to the feeding and is essentially an active sourdough starter once again.

IMPACT OF SOURDOUGH ON BREAD SHELF LIFE

The longer shelf life in bread was possibly associated to the higher water binding capacity of flour, lower crumb firmness, higher loaf volume and bread potentials to prevent microbial contaminations. The sourdough ecosystem has earned special interest due to the benefits gained by its use in bread making. The use of sourdough in bread making contributes to the improvement of bread physical and microbiological shelf life compared to straight doughs.

Many researchers have been studied the effect of sourdough on bread shelf life. For example, Katina (2005) studied the effects of sourdough as a tool for the improving texture and shelf life of wheat bread. She found that wheat bread flavour and texture were effectively modified using optimized sourdough. Katina et al. (2006) evaluated the effects of sourdough and enzymes on staling of high fiber wheat bread. They observed least changes in crumb firmness and rigidity of polymers in sourdough bread with enzymes. In contrast to white wheat bread, the starch granules were very much swollen in sourdough bran bread with enzyme mixture. This was hypothesized to be due to the higher water content of bread and degradation of cell wall components leading to altered distribution of water among starch, gluten and bran particles during storage. Corsetti et al. (2007) studied the effects of sourdough lactic acid bacteria on bread firmness and staling. Mentioned researchers found that the addition of sourdough to wheat bread reduced crumb firmness and slowed down firming in comparison with breads made with no addition of sourdough. Dal Bello et al. (2007) evaluated improvement of the quality and shelf life of wheat bread by fermentation with the antifungal strain Lactobacillus plantarum. They reported that sourdoughs and breads produced with this strain showed consistent ability to retard the growth of mould spoilage microorganisms. Author evaluated sourdough effect on Iranian Barbari bread staling (Sadeghi et al., 2007) and microbiological shelf life (Sadeghi et al., 2008). In our researches, significant effect of sourdough process conditions on Barbari bread staling and microbiological shelf life was clarified. Based on these results, sourdough processes for improve Barbari bread shelf life were designed and regression models for evaluation bread shelf life were exhibited.

Generally, bread shelf life is normally limited by physiochemical deterioration called staling, leading to a hard and crumbly texture and a loss of fresh bake flavour. Bread stales largely as a result of physical changes that occur in the starch-protein matrix of bread crumb. Even though starch retrogradation has been shown to be the primary cause of bread firming, other factors such as the state of proteins and the water content of dough affect the staling rate. Retrogradation is the process by which starch amylopectin reverts to a more ordered state after gelatinization. During sourdough fermentation, lactic acid bacteria produce a number of metabolites which have been shown to have a positive effect on the texture and staling of bread, e.g., organic acids, exopolysaccharides (EPS) and enzymes. EPS produced by LAB have the potential to replace more expensive hydrocolloids used as bread improvers. Recently the ability of certain sourdough originated LAB for producing EPS was demonstrated, many of which are potential anti staling substances. LAB strains possessing proteolytic and amylolytic properties were most effective in delaying staling. Organic acids affect the protein and starch fractions of flour. Additionally, the drop in pH associated with acid production causes an increase in the proteases and amylases activity of the flour, thus leading to a reduction in staling.

The influence of sourdough on bread staling is partly based on improved volume and a positive correlation has been established between softness and volume. The acidity level of sourdough and subsequent bread dough seems to be an important factor. This might be partly explained by the formation of low molecular weight dextrins in acidic conditions, which have been postulated to interfere with the starch retrogradation process. On the other hand, sourdough has been reported to reduce starch hydrolysis by inhibiting endogenous flour alfa amylases. Also, the solubilisation of arabinoxylans during sourdough fermentation might reduce bread staling as pentosans have been postulated to prevent starch-gluten interactions responsible for staling.

It has been noted, however, that the anti staling effect seen for sourdough is strain specific, involving dynamics other than those associated with the degree of acidification. Activities associated with bacterial hydrolysis of starch and the proteolysis of gluten subunits have been proposed by Corsetti et al. (1998), Katina (2005), Katina et al. (2006) and Sadeghi et al. (2007).

With respect to deterioration in the quality of bread during shelf life, mould growth is the most common cause of microbial spoilage. In addition to the economic losses associated with spoilage of this nature, another concern is the possibility that mycotoxins produced by the moulds may cause public health problems. Sourdough capable to control and inhibition of spoilage organisms during fermentation, due to different factors especially low pH value. Positive effects of the use of sourdough on the mould-free shelf life of wheat bread have been reported. Certain sourdough lactic acid bacteria and their components have been shown to have an antifungal effect against various fungal species isolated from flour and bakery products. The same effect has been demonstrated in the context of sourdough wheat breads. The fungi static effect of sourdough addition is attributed to organic acid produced by the LAB strains.

Sourdough addition is the most promising procedure to preserve bread from spoilage, since it is in agreement with the consumer demand for natural and additive-free food products.

It is evident that the antifungal phenomenon is not only due to the development of organic acids during the sourdough fermentation process. No correlation between bread shelf life and pH level was reported, but the type and amount of acid present may have an effect on other microstatic agents. The antifungal activities of lactic acid bacteria are complex and that the presence of organic acids may indeed play a role. Other substances contributing to activity of this nature may include reuterin, hydroxyl fatty acids, proteinaceous compounds, cyclic dipeptides, 3-phenyllactic acid, caproic acid, diacetyl and hydrogen peroxide (Messens and De Vuyst, 2002; Clarke and Arendt, 2005; Simsek et al., 2006; Dal Bello et al., 2007).

Rope spoilage is the most important spoilage of bread after mouldiness. Ropiness in bread is usually caused by Bacillus sp. This spoilage is initially noticed as an unpleasant odour, followed by a discoloured, sticky soft bread crumb caused by the breakdown of starch and proteins by microbial amylases and proteases and by the production of extracellular, slimy polysaccharides.

One effective means to limit the germination and growth of rope forming bacteria is to increase acidity, which creates an unfavorable environment for the survival of endospores. Acidity can be increased by adding acidulants or by sourdough fermentation. The most effective acids are propionic acid and acetic acid. Lactic acid has been reported to be less effective. Lactic acid bacteria can also produce antimicrobial compounds (bacteriocins; that are low molecular mass peptides or proteins with a bactericidal or bacteriostatic mode of action) such as nisin, which have the potential to inhibit germination and the growth of Bacillus species. The antimicrobial activity of sourdough arises from lactic acid, acetic acid, carbon dioxide, diacetyl, ethanol, hydrogen peroxide and bacteriocins produced by lactic acid bacteria during fermentation. Bacteriocin producing Lactobacillus strains can play a significant role in preventing rope formation in bread by the addition of sourdough prepared by these strains. However, lactic acid bacteria with a capability to produce bacteriocins have not been very effective in sourdough breads and the inhibitory effect of sourdough has been reported to be mainly due to the production of acids (Messens and De Vuyst, 2002; Katina et al., 2002; Mentes et al., 2007; Sadeghi et al., 2008).

The application of sourdough confers many advantages on the shelf life of the baked goods produced. The prospect of increasing shelf life of breads is considerable economic impact and favorable from a consumer`s perspective. In this regard, it is to be anticipated that the considerable resources that have been devoted to the biotechnology of lactic acid bacteria over the past number of years will deliver results with respect to this objective.

Starter Basics

A starter is a mixture of flour and water that has the yeast and bacteria needed to make sourdough. Feeding it with more flour and water (called "freshening it") keeps the starter active. This feeding accomplishes several things:

It feeds the yeast and bacteria in the starter to keep them healthy.

The bacteria makes the starter slightly acidic, which discourages mold and gives the baked goods their flavor.

It ensures more starter is available for use in recipes (and for sharing with others).

The amounts of flour and water used to freshen a starter can vary. I normally use equal volumes of flour and water, which makes a starter that is thin enough to pour. I have also seen recipes that use equal weights of flour and water, which is about 2 cups of flour to each cup of water. While I'm sure either mixture could be used, the amounts of flour and water in a recipe need adjustment depending on which ratio is used to freshen your starter.

There are several ways to get a sourdough starter:

If you know someone who already has some, you could ask for a little of their starter after they have freshened it. The advantage to this is that you have someone with sourdough experience who can help you out if you have any questions.

There are several companies that sell starters (an online search will turn up some possibilities). Many of these are from starters that people have passed down for many years, and some claim that they are "descended" from those used during the California or the Alaskan Gold Rushes!

You can create your own starter, as explained in the next section.

Instructions

Creating your own starter takes a little time, but it's not difficult. This could take a week or so before you have a starter that is ready for use in baking, so don't plan on starting this afternoon and serving a wonderful loaf of sourdough bread for dinner!

Start with a clean, non-metal container (preferably glass), and a non-metal mixing spoon. Metal containers and spoons can give your starter an off-flavor if they are in contact for too long. The container should be at least 1 quart in size so the starter has room to bubble up and expand.

Mix 2 cups of flour and 2 cups of water (non-chlorinated) until you have a smooth paste. Stir in 1 package of dry yeast.

Cover the container with a dishcloth or cover to keep out contaminants (other yeasts, mold, etc), but the cover should not be airtight. While the yeast is working, it will give off carbon dioxide that needs to escape.

Leave the covered container in a warm, draft-free area. Stir the mixture daily.

When there is a pleasant sour aroma, and the initial activity has decreased, you can freshen the starter by adding equal volumes of flour and water.

This process usually takes about 1 week, but it can vary depending on temperatures and other factors.

What Tools Do You Need?

I don't recommend you worry too much about having all of the bells and whistles but if you were to splurge on a few things, here is what I would recommend:

Scale

The first and most used thing you will need is a good scale. All of my recipes are weighed in grams and it makes it much easier for a baker to use the weight of ingredients

Containers

You'll need a variety of containers and tubs for your starter and doughs. This makes it easy for you when you want to mix and ferment your dough.

Proofing Baskets

Proofing baskets help if you aren't confident enough in your shaping to let your loaves proof on a cutting board or sheet pan.

Loaf Pans

Loaf tins are great for your enriched breads or any old dough that you don't want to waste and want to bake.

WHAT MAKES SOURDOUGH SPECIAL?

Ask anyone who's eaten sourdough and they'll tell you that the tang is what makes it special. I agree, and in fact the signature tartness of sourdough bread comes from the same bacteria that gives yogurt and sour cream their pucker too. It's found naturally in wheat flour, along with yeast, and comes to life when the flour is mixed with water. Here's a very simple explanation of the process:

wheat flour + water –> natural enzymes break down starches into glucose (sugar)

natural bacteria (tang) + glucose –> food for natural yeast

natural yeast + food –> natural leaven (carbon dioxide)

natural leaven + more flour + more water –> more natural leaven

So basically you start with flour and water. Nature takes its course and over time, you have a mixture that contain enough leaven (yeast) to make bread rise. Pretty cool, right? Who knew doing so little could yield such an amazing result!

Why should we eat sourdough bread?

Given that these breads are produced in large quantities and are made in just a few hours, they are not allowed to undergo an adequate process of fermentation and end up being lesser products, both in terms of their smell, taste and texture, and in terms of their nutritional value. When bread is allowed to ferment slowly, the chains of gluten are broken down more thoroughly, meaning that the human body can digest it more easily. Because of this, gluten-sensitive people can eat such handmade breads without suffering serious reactions to the gluten: the glycemic index of these foods is considerably lower given the reduction of carbohydrates in the dough.

The bread's taste and smell are given during the fermentation process, in which the yeast and bacteria consume carbohydrates (which take the form of sugar in the flour), creating acids (which are responsible for the smell and taste of the bread), ethanol and carbonic gas. In the making of the bread the processes of alcoholic fermentation (which occurs in the making of alcoholic beverages) and acetic fermentation (which turns said alcohol into acid) take place. On the other hand, lactic fermentation results in tastier and more durable foods. As such, the process according to which these foods are made has a direct influence on the consistency, aeration and lightness of the dough. If the fermentation process is long and controlled the acids, ethanol and carbonic gas will abound and the bread will be better.

Those first bubbles were almost a revelation. A couple of days before, I had mixed together flour and water into a paste. But now pockets of gas percolated through that seemingly inert glob. It was breathing. It was alive.

This gloppy mess, exuding a whiff of vinegar, was my nascent sourdough starter. When mature, it would be a pungent brew of yeasts and bacteria, a complex ecosystem that would hopefully yield delicious loaves of sourdough bread.

As the microbes eat the sugars in the flour, they exhale carbon dioxide, producing the bubbles that turn a flat, dense loaf into something light and fluffy. A starter breathes life into bread. If the loaf is the body, the starter is the soul.

Within is something magical and mysterious. Passed down through generations, starters carry tradition, history and nostalgia. People give them names like Lazarus and Clint Yeastwood. They deliver layers of flavors and aromas, the products of countless microorganisms — some whose identities and activities remain undiscovered.

Sourdough starter that is 2 days old.

unknowingly joined a growing trend. More home bakers are now eating and baking sourdough, popularized by professionals like Chad Robertson of Tartine in San Francisco. (He and others have also been experimenting with new types of grains, milling their own heirloom and ancient varieties for flavor and nutrition.)Love Your

Sourdough Starter? In Stockholm, You Can Hire A Sitter For It

THE SALT

Love Your Sourdough Starter? In Stockholm, You Can Hire A Sitter For It

According to sourdough lovers, its advantages are three-fold. The bread lasts longer, thanks to microbes that produce acids and antibiotic compounds, preventing spoilage. Evidence also suggests sourdough is better for digestion.

And, most importantly, it tastes better.

But there's nothing new about sourdough. It has been around for millennia, since the first bakers — perhaps in the Middle East — noticed that, after a couple of days, their gruel of grains and water started to bubble. Nearly all leavened bread in the world came from sourdough: from the French baguette to the Chinese mantou, from East African injera to the famous San Francisco sourdough, developed at Boudin bakery in 1849. Sourdough doesn't have to be sour, and the term simply refers to any bread made from wild yeasts and bacteria.

Today's store-bought bread relies on commercial yeast, a single species called Saccharomyces cerevisiae. Food scientists first isolated and developed it in the 19th century for its consistency and fast-rising times. But not taste.

Sourdough starters, though, vary widely. You can make and maintain one with only wheat flour and water. Others use ingredients like rye flour, milk, grapes or potatoes.

While packaged, commercial yeast can sit in your cupboard for a couple of years, a sourdough starter is more like a pet or a high-maintenance houseplant. You have to feed it regularly, or, if you're away, check it into a sourdough hotel. Properly maintained, a starter can live indefinitely, and some have purportedly persisted for centuries.

The author's starter showing the bubbles starting to form. Woo first mixed it up on Jan. 20, 2016, and has maintained it since. In this photo, the starter was close to its peak.

Marcus Woo for NPR

For Rachel Poulsen's family, a sourdough starter — fed with flour and evaporated milk — was important enough to serve as a wedding gift, passed down two generations starting from her great-grandfather, Leo V. Jolley Sr. He first got the starter from a sheep camp in Provo, Utah, which likely got it from Mormon settlers in the late 1800s. Her mom made sourdough pancakes every Sunday. "I almost feel like I'm addicted to sourdough," says Poulsen, who now lives in East Palo Alto, Calif. "I can keep eating them; I crave them."

Carina Westling of Brighton, U.K., got her rye starter 25 years ago in Sweden from a friend. Her friend's family had taken it with them when they fled Estonia in World War II, the starter being vigorous enough to have eaten through its bag during the journey. Before then, the starter had been in the family for perhaps more than 150 years. "It's not my tradition, but I've been honored to carry a part of that tradition forward," Westling says.

The family starter was one of the few things Liz Terhune packed in her car when she moved across country to Las Vegas. "It's a family heirloom to me," she says. "It's more important to me than things." Her great-aunt, who got the starter in the 1950s from a crab fisherman in Alaska, used to make sourdough pancakes for her and her sister during the summer. The starter likely originates from at least the late 1800s, Terhune says.

If you want a starter with a unique pedigree, you can buy it from places like Sourdough International, which has collected starters from bakers around the world, from Saudi Arabia to New Zealand. Each one, the company says, features its own distinct flavor.

Some say a starter's microbial community changes — and so does its flavor— once you bring it to a different environment. "There's no reason for people to go chasing special pedigrees," says Sandor Katz, author of the Art of Fermentation. "It's going to be all about what you feed it and the technique of how often you're feeding it."

The truth is, no one knows for sure, says Rob Dunn, a biologist at North Carolina State University. Lab experiments have revealed the basic biochemistry of sourdough, but no one has yet explored the diversity found in the real world.

"What food scientists have mainly been about is the average story, but not understanding the variation — even though what eating is about is the beauty of that variation," Dunn says. "We know enough to ask really good questions, but we don't know enough to know the answers."

That is why Dunn is starting the Sourdough Project. He and other researchers are soliciting home bakers to submit their starters for analysis. By sequencing the starters' DNA, the researchers can assemble a census of sourdough biodiversity and analyze variations in pH levels, enzyme production and other aspects of its biochemistry.

How does it affect the starter if you feed it milk instead of water? How does the feeding schedule influence the microbes? Do geography and climate matter? Or, whether the baker is a man or woman? Women, Dunn tells me, tend to have more bacteria called lactobacilli on their bodies.

Flour and water on the left; just starter on the right.

Courtesy of Lea Shell/Sourdough Project

To see how individual differences manifest themselves in bread, the researchers plan a big bake-off next summer. They will get 20 bakers together, sequence their DNA (as well as the microbes on their bodies), and have them make starters and bake bread, then compare the results. The goal is to see whether different people with different genetics and different microbes on their bodies have any effect on the starters.

Ultimately, Dunn says, the researchers want to identify which microorganisms make the best-tasting loaf. Ideally, they'll bake thousands of loaves with different starters and enlist chefs and bakers to judge.

"If we know what's in [a starter], we can predict what abilities it might have, what flavors it might have," he says. "For me, that's kind of a fun one, because all that flavor stuff is super magical and not very quantitative, and yet it's measurable."

It will still be months before answers start to trickle in. First, the researchers need samples to study. I'll submit my starter, and if you want to help as well, visit their page.

Meanwhile, I still get a kick out of seeing those bubbles. Replenishing fresh flour and water turns my starter back into a bland mush. But a few hours later, the bubbles return, the mass puffs up in volume, the aromas waft, and the starter springs back to life. It really is like magic, only better. It's biochemistry.

How To Make Sourdough Bread Last Longer

Never know the best way to store bread? If stored properly, traditional sourdough bread (the proper stuff that is, that's been fermented slowly and is full of natural acidity) can last four to five days.

Founder of BreadBread bakery in Brixton, Bridget Hugo has been working with slow 24-hour fermentation since she created the sourdough pizza base at Franco Manca. Here she reveals her expert tips for storing your sourdough bread loaf and keep it fresher for longer.Did you know, the natural acidity of sourdough bread discourages bacteria, so it takes longer than yeasted bread to develop mould? Each loaf baked at BreadBread is a ‘slow’ product. It’s been treated with respect and given ample time to develop into the tastiest, most digestible bread. Our slow-made sourdough is particularly stable, which means it keeps especially well.

The best way to store bread is…

Ideally, you should store your loaf in a cotton bread bag or wrapped in a large tea towel, so that the bread can ‘breathe’. Leave your bread in a relatively cool place so it can maintain normal ambient moisture levels.

It is not recommended to store bread in the fridge. A fridge is an extremely dry environment and will harden the bread quickly.

Storing bread in a plastic bag is also not ideal particularly in a warm place as the bag may cause 'sweating'. Moisture and warmth encourages bacteria.

If you have several loaves to store, wrap them in clingfilm and put in a cool place. For longer term storage place cling-wrapped bread in the freezer.

Try re-baking your bread

No bread is ever 'fresh' for long. The loveliest bread is eaten just-cooled, about 2 to 6 hours after it has been removed from the oven. After that, the crust will become either soft and flakey, or dry and brittle or simply tough and dull – depending on the bread type and age of the bread.Not everyone is lucky enough to live near a bakery offering fresh loaves. However, you can replicate that fresh-out-the-oven experience simply by re-baking your loaf in your oven at home, a much-overlooked trick! Though easy to execute, it takes a bit of planning.

Surprisingly, it takes about the same length of time to re-bake bread as it takes to bake bread from the raw dough, albeit at a much lower temperature. You also need to time for the loaf to cool down again. Hot bread, like crazy paving, is not all it is cracked up to be. The starches, when heated, revert to their original state and are less digestible, so you should leave it at least one hour to cool. This means you will need to get your bread in the oven a couple of hours before you need it.

Re-baking your loaf both refreshes your bread and your options on how you use or present it

How to re-bake your sourdough loaf

For loaves that are a few days old, preheat your oven to 200°C. Spray the crust all round with water, then re-bake on the middle rack for 30-50 minutes, depending on the size of the loaf:

1kg (or less) loaves / pieces 30-40 minutes

1kg (or more) loaves / pieces 40-50 minutes

For whole or sliced bread loaves that are frozen, allow the loaf to defrost first. There is no need to spray them.

If your bread has already been sliced, wrap it firmly in tin foil before baking it. You can open the top up about 10 minutes before you remove it to improve crustiness.

Ideas for using stale bread

You can smear all sides of sliced breads with flavoured butters before wrapping them in foil to bake. The obvious choice for this is a freshly-made garlic butter, but you can also use a herb butter made with parsley or oregano and even creamed nut butters.

You can slather your slices with pesto instead of butter. Many good pestos are available ready-made or you can make your own, with olive oil and herbs of your choice plus optional hard cheeses and nuts or seeds. Almost any filling, as long as it is more oily than wet, will work.

If you want to make toast with hot toppings, try baking your slices instead of toasting them, with the topping already on top, bruschetta style.

You guys know the health benefits of yogurt and kefir, right? Imagine those benefits, fresh and warm from the oven and smeared with butter.

LACTOBACILLUS

Lactobacillus is the good bacteria in yogurt, kefir, sour cream, buttermilk, etc. It ferments the flour/water mixture and creates lactic acid, a catalyst that greatly increases the micronutrient profile. In simple terms – all those nutrients found in whole wheat flour are bigger and badder, and now your body is better able to USE them too.

The fermentation process alone is great for your digestive system. The Lactobacillus helps feed the good bacteria found in your digestive system so they can continue to fight off the bad guys. And remember that a healthy gut means healthy body. Most of your immune system is found in your digestive system.

PHYTATES

One neat thing to the long soaking required of sourdough is that it breaks down much of the phytates that bind the awesome minerals in grains. With the phytates gone, our bodies can grab those nutrients and actually use them!

With those nutrients readily available, digestion of the starch is MUCH easier on your body. In fact, the natural bacteria working with the natural yeast predigests the starch a little bit for you. The benefits of sourdough will make your tummy happy.

GLUCOSE

Remember how the natural yeast feeds on the glucose? With a large portion of the glucose devoured in the fermentation process, sourdough doesn't cause a spike in your blood sugars like processed white breads often do. The long process also breaks down many of the gluten proteins into amino acids, possibly making sourdough bread tolerable for those who are sensitive to gluten!

One last neat tid-bit: sourdough bread is less likely to stale, retains much of its moisture as it ages, and its acidity helps prevent the growth of mold! Now this doesn't mean your sourdough won't EVER go stale and will NEVER grow mold. But it's nice to know that the artisan loaf you treated yourself to at the farmer's market won't go bad too quickly.

The Key To Great Sourdough/ A Healthy Sourdough Starter!

In order to make good sourdough you need an active sourdough starter. This means not thinking you can feed your starter for 1 day and thinking that your bread is gonna be great. By keeping an active starter, feeding it once a day, ideally twice a day, and that will give the best and most consistent results. If you're not making bread a lot, all you have to do is feed your starter once a week and place it in the fridge.

I’m telling you I get so many pictures of beginners loaf’s that don't come out great, and many times its due to a weak starter. Keep it consistent.

Also, don't throw away your starter! Your sourdough starter from the night before isn’t super powerful but it has a great flavor. So pour your sourdough starter into a pan on medium heat with some oil in it and let that fry. Before you flip it, sprinkling it with some sesame seeds, scallion, and any seasoning you want. Flip it over and then cook it for another 4 - 5 minutes. This is delicious for breakfast or just a side snack!

Now back to my starter, we want 150 grams total so i'm going to feed it with equal parts water and plain white flour at 75 grams each. Let that sit out at room temp for 3-5 hours until its reaches its max height and activity, in the meantime we can move onto the next step.

Don't Forget Autolyse:

This step is just to combine the water and flour and develop which instantly starts to develop gluten bonds in the dough without doing any work.

You want to autolyse for at least 45 minutes but whole wheat will take a little longer. You can even do it overnight if you want but 45 minutes is a good time.

Using Baker's Percentages.

Most recipes for sourdough bread is in baker's percentage because they come from bakeries. Bakers percentages make its super easy to expand on your bread recipe which is necessary in bakeries.

Understanding bakers percentages is super easy, if you have 1000 grams of flour, and you want a hydration level of 80 percent that means the amount of hydration or the wetness of your dough, you just take 80 percent of your flour, which is 800. So the percentage is always related to the amount of flour.

Another great thing about bakers percentage is that you can add any amount of flour on a scale. So in this case, my goal is 1000 grams of flour but I am going to add different flours

Lowering Your Hydration Level:

Most recipes will get you a hydration level around 80 percent, which is great for a super airy loaf, but sourdough is so tricky to work with since its a wet dough, not like pizza dough! I generally recommend that experienced or beginners bakers start closer to a 70 - 75 percent hydration so they don't run into a "sticky situation" later in the process and lose all your confidence. You bread bakers out there know what I'm talking about!

Now that we have our flour weighed out, I'm going to zero out my scale and add my 750 grams of water, to get to 78 percent hydration.

When To Use Your Starter:

The starter will generally take 3 - 6 hours to be fully active but no recipe is going to tell you when your starter is ready, this is live fermentation! You have to use your intuition. You want to pull it when its at its peak. When a sourdough starter is at its peak it should have a rounded top and double in size. If it collapses it means it has run out of food and it has been over proofed. Check out the time-lapse of my sourdough starter here!

Another technique is the float test. Generally, I don't do this but doing a float test will give you more security when know when you can use your starter.

Add 150 grams of starter and 20 grams salt but just make sure the salt is fine so that it dissolves into the dough. Then stretch and fold in your starter and salt until everything is combined. The dough will not be perfectly smooth since the salt has not dissolved. Your goal here is just to incorporate everything.

Never Knead Your Sourdough Shake, Pull, & Fold Instead:

Alright so we are officially active, fermentation begins once that starter hits more food! Food being this fresh flour and water you now have supplies it with. This was when we start the stretch and fold process. Which brings us to tip 6. Never knead your dough, were not making pizza dough, we want an airy crumb and by stretching and folding your dough, you are aligning the gluten strands without removing gas built up from the fermentation.

Extensibility - you can stretch the dough without it breaking vs. Elasticity - stretching the dough and it will come back

You will be doing the shake, pull, and fold method every 30 minutes for 2 hours.

How Do You Know When To Finish Working The Dough?

Once every half hour you will give your dough a stretch and fold. Every single time the texture of your dough will change. It will start to look a little bit more shiny, a little smoother, and little more supple as you continue to stretch and fold. If you look at the outside edges of the dough in your bowl, every time the shape should get a little more round because your continuing to align the gluten strands and build a stronger gluten structure.

By the 4th stretch and fold your dough should be looking a hell of a lot nicer and should feel much better than when you started the process.

Let The Dough Proof On Your Schedule.

Even though bread making is a long process, there's ways to actually slow down the fermentation to work around your schedule.

How can a slower fermentation be better for me? Well there's two specific times where you can slow down the fermentation to work within your schedule.

Once you dough is finished stretching and folding, it's looking great! Now we have to let it bulk rise at this point. That could take place at room temp for 2-5 hours, but since im making this at night, I don't have that time, so I'm gonna throw this puppy in the fridge and slow down the femrnation so it will be ready to go in the morning. If you do have time to bulk rise at room temp then you can just go for it and let it gain some volume and expand for a few hours.

Well, when you slow down the fermenting process, the bread rises slower because yeast isn’t as active in cold temps but the bacteria in the dough is still active so you can get more flavor!

Don't Use Too Much Flour! Bench Scrapers Are Friends.

Once your dough has finished the bulk rising process, you will see some nice bubbles forms from the fermentation process, you should also smell some of that dough fermentation in action. Now we're gonna pre shape our loaves and let them bench rest which takes us to tip 9, dealing with a wet dough! It is one of the trickiest parts about making sourdough bread, most people aren't used to a high hydrated dough so getting right texture of stickiness to dryness of your dough is key. This blance is huge and takes a while to get right, I stilll fuck it up all the time.

A lot of people freak out and start adding too much flour at this stage, but if its too dry, then it won't stick together to shape it and of course if it’s too sticky, well then your gonna have a sticky situation which isn't fun.

Dust your work surface with a little bit of flour. It will be a little hard to handle since it is a wet dough. Your best friend in this process will be your bench scraper, which wont stick to the dough so you don't have to add too much flour, think of it like a non stick hand...

Cut your dough in half and give it a quick preshape. Let the two dough balls sit on your floured surface for 30 minutes. In this step you really just want to get it into a round ball and then let the gluten relax again so that when you give it the final preshape it's easier to get it into a cleaner shape.

However, if after 20 minutes they flatten out/sunk that means that they didn't get the proper gluten development.

Generously Flour Your Banneton

Your dough is ready to be placed into a banneton so flour the banneton generously. You can overcompensate the flour in this step because you can always dust it off later and you don't want your dough to stick to the banneton. If you’d like, you can use a duster to help give you an even coating of flour.

At this point if you want to have some seeds or grains on top place them onto your work surface and roll the dough onto the plate filled with your seeds. If your dough isn't sticky enough then the seeds/grains won't stick so in this case you should mist a little bit of water on top of the dough to create some tackiness. If you don't feel like adding in any seeds/grains you are ready to let your dough rest for the last time!

There's No Perfect Way To Shape Your Dough

Once the 30 minutes are up you can now beginning to shape your dough for the last time. Lightly flour your surface one more time and lightly tap it into a square. Grab the two closest corners near you and fold one corner on top of the other corner. Repeat this until you get to the other side of the dough.

Then come back to the side of the dough nearest you and start to roll the dough up into a wide log. The dough should already be seam side down so let it rest for about 15 seconds just so that the seam seals up. If it helps to watch, you can see me do this here.

It’s good to know that there is no perfect way to shape your bread. Just because this is how I shape my bread doesn't mean you can find your own method that works for you. I've been in bakeries and have seen so many different techniques. Your main objective of shaping is to roll a tight loaf with some nice surface tension without taking the air out of it but it will still has a good surface tension!

Place your loaf into the banneton and give it another sprinkling of flour. The bread will rise into the side of the proofing basket so you want to make sure that you flour the edges of the bread as well. Finally, let your dough rest in a cool shady spot for 3 -5 hours or you can let it proof overnight if you'd like. Either way, 45 minutes before you are ready to bake preheat your oven and your dutch pan can anywhere from 500 to 550 degrees.

The No Fail Poke Test

Once your bread has rested and you think its ready but you just aren't sure yet, you can always give it the poke test! The poke test is the best way to tell if your bread is ready to go in the oven or not and it's super simple method. Once your bread has rested, give it a poke about 1 inch deep. If it springs back then it needs more time. If it doesn't bounce back it means that it is over proofed but if you give it a poke and it bounces back but leaves a dent then it’s perfect. You are now one step closer to eating your delicious sourdough loaf!

Baking Trays Prevent Burnt Bottoms

Once your bread has passed the poke test, grab a parchment paper and place it on of the banneton and flip the bread out being careful to not knock too much air out in the process. Brush off the excess flour so that it doesn't burn and give it a slash with a lame. Now, carefully place your bread into the dutch oven being aware of where your hands are so that you don't burn yourself. Let the loaf bake for 20 minutes.

Once the 20 minutes are up continue baking the dough for another 20 minutes except drop the temperature to 450 degrees fahrenheit and place a baking tray under the dutch oven. This is to prevent any burning on the bottom while allowing the crust to caramelize and develop even more flavor!

Go Off Color Not Time

Even though my recipe say 20 minutes it's important to know that it's not always about time. Look at the color of the bread, you are looking for a charred dark brown crust. So after 20 minutes give your bread a look is it too pale? Do you need more time? Is it just right? If it's too blonde add another 15 minutes and check again once the timer goes off. Check out how I like the color of my bread here.

Here’s an awesome bonus tip for ya! Instead of taking out the bread at the end for 20 minutes, leave it in, crack the oven open just a bit, and this will dry out the crust. This step adds a whole new depth of flavor to your sourdough!

It’s Okay If You Fail Miserably

If you failed miserably don't be too hard on yourself. Sourdough is a hard artform to get right especially when every step needs to be perfect. Keep trying and I promise you'll get it right and it will all be worth it when that beautiful sourdough loaf comes out of the oven!

Not everyone agrees that sourdough microbial communities are so variable. In commercial bakers' sourdoughs, which are fed daily or even more often, the microbes always have plenty of food. That creates a race, with the fastest-reproducing microbes dominating over time, says Michael Gänzle, a food microbiologist at the University of Alberta, Canada. In the long run, he says, the winners are the yeast Kazachstania and the lactic acid bacterium Lactobacillus sanfranciscensis (recently renamed Fructilactobacillus sanfranciscensis) .That's not necessarily good news for the resulting bread: L. sanfranciscensis grows fastest because it has one of the smallest genomes among lactic acid bacteria, which means it has fewer metabolic pathways and thus fewer flavor-producing by-products than other bacteria, Gänzle says. (Score one for home sourdoughs, which Landis says might be more diverse.)

But the flavor of a sourdough bread depends on more than just the species of microbes present in the starter. “You can have really different sourdoughs even if the microflora is the same,” says Lacaze. “It depends also on the recipe of the sourdough, the parameters of the culture.” Stiffer starters — that is, those made with a lower proportion of water — trap more oxygen within the dough, and this encourages lactic acid bacteria to produce sharper-tasting acetic acid; in runnier starters, the same bacteria produce softer-tasting lactic acid.

www.ingramcontent.com/pod-product-compliance
Ingram Content Group UK Ltd.
Pitfield, Milton Keynes, MK11 3LW, UK
UKHW021918190726
13853UKWH00002B/732